The Five Mental Hindrances and Their Conquest

Selected Texts from the Pali Canon and the Commentaries

Compiled and translated by

Nyanaponika Thera

Buddhist Publication Society
54 Sangharaja Mawatha
PO Box 61, Kandy
Sri Lanka
http://www.bps.lk

First BPS edition: 1961
Reprinted: 1973, 1984, 1993, 2013, 2018

ISBN: 978-955-24-0111-4

Printed by
Ruchira Offset Printers
Kandy—Sri Lanka

CONTENTS

Introduction

Unshakable deliverance of the mind is the highest goal in the Buddha's doctrine. Here, deliverance means: the freeing of the mind from all limitations, fetters, and bonds that tie it to the Wheel of Suffering, to the Circle of Rebirth. It means: the cleansing of the mind of all defilements that mar its purity; the removing of all obstacles that bar its progress from the mundane (*lokiya*) to the supramundane consciousness (*lokuttara-citta*), that is, to Arahatship.

Many are the obstacles which block the road to spiritual progress, but there are five in particular which, under the name of hindrances (*nivaraṇa*), are often mentioned in the Buddhist scriptures:

1. Sensual desire (*kāmacchanda*),
2. Ill-will (*byāpāda*),
3. Sloth and torpor (*thīna-middha*),
4. Restlessness and remorse (*uddhacca-kukkucca*),
5. Sceptical doubt (*vicikicchā*).

They are called "hindrances" because they hinder and envelop the mind in many ways, obstructing its development (*bhāvanā*). According to the Buddhist teachings, spiritual development is twofold: through tranquillity (*samatha-bhāvanā*) and through insight (*vipassanā-bhāvanā*). Tranquillity is gained by complete concentration of the mind during the meditative absorptions (*jhāna*). For achieving these absorptions, the overcoming of the five hindrances, at least temporarily, is a preliminary condition. It is especially in the context of achieving the absorptions that the Buddha often mentions the five hindrances in his discourses.

There are five mental constituents which are chiefly representative of the first meditative absorption, and are therefore called the factors of absorption (*jhānaṅga*). For each of these there is, according to Buddhist commentarial tradition, one of the five hindrances that is specifically harmful for it and excludes its higher development and refinement to the degree required for jhāna; and on the other hand, the cultivation of these five factors beyond their average level will be an antidote against the hindrances, preparing the road to jhāna. The relationship between these two groups of five is indicated in this anthology, under the heading of the respective hindrance.

Not only the meditative absorptions but also lesser degrees of mental concentration are impeded by these five hindrances. So is the "neighbourhood" (or "access") concentration (*upacārasamādhi*), being the preliminary stage for the fully absorbed concentration (*appanā*) reached in jhāna. Likewise excluded by the presence of the hindrances is the momentary concentration (*khaṇikasamādhi*) which has the strength of neighbourhood concentration and is required for mature insight (*vipassanā*). But apart from these higher stages of mental development, any earnest attempt at clear thinking and pure living will be seriously affected by the presence of these five hindrances.

This widespread harmful influence of the five hindrances shows the urgent necessity of breaking down their power by constant effort. One should not believe it sufficient to turn one's attention to the hindrances only at the moment when one sits down for meditation. Such last-minute effort in suppressing the hindrances will rarely be successful unless helped by previous endeavour during one's ordinary life.

One who earnestly aspires to the unshakable deliverance of the mind should, therefore, select a definite "working-ground" of a direct and practical import: a *kammaṭṭhāna*[1] in its widest sense, on which the structure of his entire life should be based. Holding fast to that "working-ground," never losing sight of it for long, even this alone will be a considerable and encouraging progress in the control and development of the mind, because in that way the directive and purposive energies of mind will be strengthened considerably. One who has chosen the conquest of the five hindrances for a "working-ground" should examine which of the five are strongest in one's personal case. Then one should carefully observe how, and on which occasions, they usually appear. One should further know the positive forces within one's own mind by which each of these hindrances can best be countered and, finally, conquered; and one should also examine one's life for any opportunity of developing these qualities which, in the following pages, have been indicated under the headings of the spiritual faculties (*indriya*), the factors of absorption (*jhānaṅga*), and the factors of enlightenment (*bojjhaṅga*). In some cases, subjects of meditation have

1. I.e., subject of meditation: literally "working-ground."

been added which will be helpful in overcoming the respective hindrances.

By the "worldling" (*puthujjana*),[2] however, only a temporary suspension and partial weakening of the hindrances can be attained. Their final and complete eradication takes place on the stages of sanctity (*ariyamagga*):

1) Doubt is eliminated on the first stage, the path of stream-entry (*sotāpatti-magga*).

1) Sensual desire, ill will and remorse are eliminated on the third stage, the path of non-returner (*anāgāmi-magga*).

2) Sloth and torpor and restlessness are eradicated on the path of Arahatship (*arahatta-magga*).

Hence the reward of the fight against the hindrances is not only the limited one of making possible a shorter or longer spell of meditation, but every step in weakening these hindrances takes us nearer to the stages of sanctity where deliverance from these hindrances is unshakable.

Though most of the following texts, translated from the Discourses of the Buddha and the commentaries, are addressed to monks, they are likewise valid for those living the worldly life. As the Old Masters say: "The monk (*bhikkhu*) is mentioned here as an example of those dedicated to the practice of the Teaching. Whosoever undertakes that practice is here included in the term 'monk.'

---

2. A "worldling," or *puthujjana*, who may be a monk or layman, is one who has not yet attained to the first stage of sanctity, the Path of stream-entry (*sotāpatti-magga*).

The Five Hindrances

I. General Texts

There are five impediments and hindrances, overgrowths of the mind that stultify insight. What five?

Sensual desire is an impediment and hindrance, an overgrowth of the mind that stultifies insight. Ill-will… Sloth and torpor… Restlessness and remorse… Sceptical doubt are impediments and hindrances, overgrowths of the mind that stultify insight.

Without having overcome these five, it is impossible for a monk whose insight thus lacks strength and power, to know his own true good, the good of others, and the good of both; nor will he be capable of realizing that superhuman state of distinctive achievement, the knowledge and vision enabling the attainment of sanctity.

But if a monk has overcome these five impediments and hindrances, these overgrowths of the mind that stultify insight, then it is possible that, with his strong insight, he can know his own true good, the good of others, and the good of both; and he will be capable of realizing that superhuman state of distinctive achievement, the knowledge and vision enabling the attainment of sanctity.

(AN 5:51)

One whose heart is overwhelmed by unrestrained covetousness will do what he should not do and neglect what he ought to do. And through that, his good name and his happiness will come to ruin.

One whose heart is overwhelmed by ill-will… by sloth and torpor… by restlessness and remorse… by sceptical doubt will do what he should not do and neglect what he ought to do. And through that, his good name and his happiness will come to ruin.

But if a noble disciple has seen these five as defilements of the mind, he will give them up. And doing so, he is regarded as one of great wisdom, of abundant wisdom, clear-visioned, well endowed with wisdom. This is called "endowment with wisdom."

(AN 4:61)

There are five impurities of gold impaired by which it is not pliant and wieldy, lacks radiance, is brittle and cannot be wrought well. What are these five impurities? Iron, copper, tin, lead and silver.

But if the gold has been freed from these five impurities, then it will be plaint and wieldy, radiant and firm, and can be wrought well. Whatever ornaments one wishes to make from it, be it a diadem, earrings, a necklace or a golden chain, it will serve that purpose.

Similarly, there are five impurities of the mind impaired by which the mind is not pliant and wieldy, lacks radiant lucidity and firmness, and cannot concentrate well upon the eradication of the taints (*āsavā*). What are these five impurities? They are: sensual desire, ill-will, sloth and torpor, restlessness and remorse, and sceptical doubt.

But if the mind is freed of these five impurities, it will be pliant and wieldy, will have radiant lucidity and firmness, and will concentrate well upon the eradication of the taints. Whatever state realizable by the higher mental faculties one may direct the mind to, one will in each case acquire the capacity of realization, if the (other) conditions are fulfilled.

(AN 5:23)

How does a monk practice mind-object contemplation on the mental objects of the five hindrances?

Herein, monks, when sensual desire is present in him the monk knows, "There is sensual desire in me," or when sensual desire is absent he knows, "There is no sensual desire in me." He knows how the arising of non-arisen sensual desire comes to be; he knows how the rejection of the arisen sensual desire comes to be; and he knows how the non-arising in the future of the rejected sensual desire comes to be.

When ill-will is present in him, the monk knows, "There is ill-will in me," or when ill-will is absent he knows, "There is no ill-will in me." He knows how the arising of non-arisen ill-will comes to be; he knows how the rejection of the arisen ill-will comes to be; and he knows how the non-arising in the future of the rejected ill-will comes to be.

When sloth and torpor are present in him, the monk knows, "There is sloth and torpor in me," or when sloth and torpor are absent he knows, "There is no sloth and torpor in me." He knows how the arising of non-arisen sloth and torpor comes to be; he knows how the rejection of the arisen sloth and torpor comes to be; and he knows how the non-arising in the future of the rejected sloth and torpor comes to be.

When restlessness and remorse are present in him, the monk knows, "There are restlessness and remorse in me," or when agitation and remorse are absent he knows, "There are no restlessness and remorse in me." He knows how the arising of non-arisen restlessness and remorse comes to be; he knows how the rejection of the arisen restlessness and remorse comes to be; and he knows how the non-arising in the future of the rejected restlessness and remorse comes to be.

When sceptical doubt is present in him, the monk knows, "There is sceptical doubt in me," or when sceptical doubt is absent he knows, "There is no sceptical doubt in me." He knows how the arising of non-arisen sceptical doubt comes to be; he knows how the rejection of the arisen sceptical doubt comes to be; and he knows how the non-arising in the future of the rejected sceptical doubt comes to be.

(MN 10; Satipaṭṭhāna Sutta)

To note mindfully, and immediately, the arising of one of the hindrances, as recommended in the preceding text, is a simple but very effective method of countering these and any other defilements of the mind. By doing so, a brake is applied against the uninhibited continuance of unwholesome thoughts, and the watchfulness of mind against their recurrence is strengthened. This method is based on a simple psychological fact which is expressed by the commentators as follows: "A good and an evil thought cannot occur in combination. Therefore, at the time of knowing the sense desire (that arose in the preceding moment), that sense desire no longer exists (but only the act of knowing)."

II. The Hindrances Individually

Just as, monks, this body lives on nourishment, lives dependent on nourishment, does not live without nourishment—in the same way, monks, the five hindrances live on nourishment, depend on nourishment, do not live without nourishment.

SN 46:2

Sensual Desire

A. Nourishment of Sensual Desire

There are beautiful objects; frequently giving unwise attention to them—this is the nourishment for the arising of sensual desire that has not arisen, and the nourishment for the increase and strengthening of sensual desire that has already arisen.

SN 46:51

B. Denourishing of Sensual Desire

There are impure objects (used for meditation); frequently giving wise attention to them—this is the denourishing of the arising of sensual desire that has not yet arisen, and the denourishing of the increase and strengthening of sensual desire that has already arisen.

SN 46:51

Commentary to the Satipaṭṭhāna Sutta

Six things are conducive to the abandonment of sensual desire:

1) Learning how to meditate on impure objects;
2) Devoting oneself to the meditation on the impure;
3) Guarding the sense doors;
4) Moderation in eating;
5) Noble friendship;
6) Suitable conversation.

1. & 2. Meditation on the impure

(a) Impure objects

In him who is devoted to the meditation about impure objects, repulsion towards beautiful objects is firmly established. This is the result.

AN 5:36

"Impure object" refers, in particular, to the cemetery meditations as given in the Satipaṭṭhāna Sutta and explained in the *Visuddhimagga*; but it refers also to the repulsive aspects of sense objects in general.

(b) The loathsomeness of the body

Herein, monks, a monk reflects on just this body, confined within the skin and full of manifold impurities from the soles upward and from the top of the hair down: "There is in this body: hair of the head, hair of the body, nails, teeth, skin, flesh, sinews, bones, marrow, kidneys, heart, liver, pleura, spleen, lungs, intestines, bowels, stomach, excrement, bile, phlegm, pus, blood, sweat, fat, tears, lymph, saliva, mucus, fluid of the joints, urine (and the brain in the skull)."

MN 10

By bones and sinews knit,
With flesh and tissue smeared,
And hidden by the skin, the body
Does not appear as it really is…
The fool thinks it beautiful,
His ignorance misguiding him…

Sutta Nipāta v. 194, 199

(c) Various contemplations

Sense objects give little enjoyment, but much pain and much despair; the danger in them prevails.

MN 14

The unpleasant overwhelms a thoughtless man in the guise of the pleasant, the disagreeable overwhelms him in the guise of the agreeable, the painful in the guise of pleasure.

Udāna 2:8

3. Guarding the sense doors

How does one guard the sense doors? Herein, a monk, having seen a form, does not seize upon its (delusive) appearance as a whole, nor on its details. If his sense of sight were uncontrolled, covetousness, grief and other evil, unwholesome states would flow into him. Therefore he practices for the sake of its control, he watches over the sense of sight, he enters upon its control. Having heard a sound… smelt an odor… tasted a taste…

felt a touch… cognized a mental object, he does not seize upon its (delusive) appearance as a whole… he enters upon its control.

SN 35:120

There are forms perceptible by the eye, which are desirable, lovely, pleasing, agreeable, associated with desire, arousing lust. If the monk does not delight in them, is not attached to them, does not welcome them, then in him thus not delighting in them, not being attached to them and not welcoming them, delight (in these forms) ceases; if delight is absent, there is no bondage. There are sounds perceptible by the ear… odors perceptible by the mind… if delight is absent, there is no bondage.

SN 35:63

4. Moderation in eating

How is he moderate in eating? Herein a monk takes his food after wise consideration: not for the purpose of enjoyment, of pride, of beautifying the body or adorning it (with muscles); but only for the sake of maintaining and sustaining this body, to avoid harm and to support the holy life, thinking: "Thus I shall destroy the old painful feeling and shall not let a new one rise. Long life will be mine, blamelessness and well-being."

MN 2; MN 39

5. Noble friendship

Reference is here, in particular, to such friends who have experience and can be a model and help in overcoming sensual desire, especially in meditating on impurity. But it applies also to noble friendship in general. The same twofold explanation holds true also for the other hindrances, with due alterations.

The entire holy life, Ānanda, is noble friendship, noble companionship, noble association. Of a monk, Ānanda, who has a noble friend, a noble companion, a noble associate, it is to be expected that he will cultivate and practice the Noble Eightfold Path.

SN 45:2

6. Suitable conversation

Reference is here in particular to conversation about the overcoming of sensual desire, especially about meditating on impurity. But it applies also to every conversation which is suitable to advance one's progress on the path. With due alterations this explanation holds true also for the other hindrances.

If the mind of a monk is bent on speaking, he (should remember this): "Talk which is low, coarse, worldly, not noble, not salutary, not leading to detachment, not to freedom from passion, not to cessation, not to tranquillity, not to higher knowledge, not to enlightenment, not to Nibbāna, namely, talk about kings, robbers and ministers, talk about armies, dangers and war, about food and drink, clothes, couches, garlands, perfumes, relatives, cars, villages, towns, cities, and provinces, about women and wine, gossip of the street and of the well, talk about the ancestors, about various trifles, tales about the origin of the world and the ocean, talk about what happened and what did not happen—such and similar talk I shall not entertain." Thus he is clearly conscious about it.

But talk about austere life, talk suitable for the unfolding of the mind, talk which is conducive to complete detachment, to freedom from passion, to cessation, tranquillity, higher knowledge, enlightenment and to Nibbāna, namely, talk about a life of frugality, about contentedness, solitude, aloofness from society, about rousing one's energy, talk about virtue, concentration, wisdom, deliverance, about the vision and knowledge of deliverance—such talk I shall entertain." Thus he is clearly conscious about it.

MN 122

These things, too, are helpful in conquering sensual desire:

3) One-pointedness of mind, of the factors of absorption (*jhānaṅga*);
4) Mindfulness, of the spiritual faculties (*indriya*);
5) Mindfulness, of the factors of enlightenment (*bojjhaṅga*).

C. Simile

If there is water in a pot mixed with red, yellow, blue or orange color, a man with a normal faculty of sight, looking into it, could not properly recognize and see the image of his own face. In the same way, when one's mind is possessed by sensual desire, overpowered by sensual desire, one cannot properly see the escape from sensual desire which has arisen; then one does not properly understand and see one's own welfare, nor that of another, nor that of both; and also texts memorized a long time ago do not come into one's mind, not to speak of those not memorized.

SN 46:55

Ill-Will

A. Nourishment of Ill-Will

There are objects causing aversion; frequently giving unwise attention to them—this is the nourishment for the arising of ill-will that has not yet arisen, and for the increase and strengthening of ill-will that has already arisen.

SN 46:51

B. Denourishing of Ill-Will

There is the liberation of the heart by loving-kindness; frequently giving wise attention to it—this is the denourishing of the arising of ill-will that has not yet arisen, and of the increase and strengthening of ill-will that has already arisen.

SN 46:51

Cultivate the meditation on loving-kindness! For by cultivating the meditation on loving-kindness, ill-will disappears.

Cultivate the meditation on compassion! For by cultivating the meditation on compassion, cruelty disappears.

Cultivate the meditation on sympathetic joy! For by cultivating the meditation on sympathetic joy, listlessness disappears.

Cultivate the meditation on equanimity! For by cultivating the meditation on equanimity, anger disappears.

MN 62

Six things are helpful in conquering ill-will:

1) Learning how to meditate on loving-kindness;
2) Devoting oneself to the meditation of loving-kindness;
3) Considering that one is the owner and heir of one's actions (*kamma*);
4) Frequent reflection on it (in the following way): Thus one should consider: "Being angry with another person, what can you do to him? Can you destroy his virtue and his other good qualities? Have you not come to your present state by your own actions, and will also go hence according to your own actions? Anger towards another is just as if someone wishing to hit another person takes hold of glowing coals, or a heated iron-rod, or of excrement. And, in the same way, if the other person is angry with you, what can he do to you? Can he destroy your virtue and your other good qualities? He too has come to his present state by his own actions and will go hence according to his own actions. Like an unaccepted gift or like a handful of dirt thrown against the wind, his anger will fall back on his own head."
5) Noble friendship;
6) Suitable conversation.

Commentary to Satipaṭṭhāna Sutta

These things, too, are helpful in conquering ill-will:

1) Rapture, of the factors of absorption (*jhānaṅga*);
2) Faith, of the spiritual faculties (*indriya*);
3) Rapture and equanimity, of the factors of enlightenment (*bojjhaṅga*).

C. Simile

If there is a pot of water heated on the fire, the water seething and boiling, a man with a normal faculty of sight, looking into it, could not properly recognize and see the image of his own face. In the same way, when one's mind is possessed by ill-will, overpowered by ill-will, one cannot properly see the escape from the ill-will which has arisen; then one does not properly understand and see one's own welfare, nor that of another, nor that of both; and also texts memorized a long time ago do not come into one's mind, not to speak of those not memorized.

SN 46:55

Sloth and Torpor

A. Nourishment of Sloth and Torpor

There arises listlessness, lassitude, lazy stretching of the body, drowsiness after meals, mental sluggishness; frequently giving unwise attention to it—this is the nourishment for the arising of sloth and torpor that have not yet arisen and for the increase and strengthening of sloth and torpor that have already arisen.

SN 46:51

B. Denourishing of Sloth and Torpor

There is the element of rousing one's energy, the element of exertion, the element of continuous exertion; frequently giving wise attention to it—this is the denourishing of the arising of sloth and torpor that have not yet arisen and of the increase and strengthening of sloth and torpor that have already arisen.

SN 46:51

"May nothing remain but skin and sinews and bones; may flesh and blood dry up in the body! Not before having achieved what can be achieved by manly strength, manly energy, manly exertion shall my energy subside!"

MN 70

Six things are conducive to the abandonment of sloth and torpor:

1) Knowing that overeating is a cause of it;
2) Changing the bodily posture;
3) Thinking of the perception of light;
4) Staying in the open air;
5) Noble friendship;
6) Suitable conversation.

These things, too, are helpful in conquering sloth and torpor:

1. Recollection of Death

To-day the effort should be made,
Who knows if tomorrow Death will come?

MN 131

2. *Perceiving the suffering in impermanence*

In a monk who is accustomed to see the suffering in impermanence and who is frequently engaged in this contemplation, there will be established in him such a keen sense of the danger of laziness, idleness, lassitude, indolence and thoughtlessness, as if he were threatened by a murderer with drawn sword.

AN 7:46

3. *Sympathetic joy*

Cultivate the meditation on sympathetic joy! For by cultivating it, listlessness will disappear.

MN 62

Applied thought, of the factors of absorptions (*jhānaṅga*); Energy, of the spiritual facilities (*indriya*); Investigation of reality, energy and rapture, of the factors of enlightenment (*bojjhaṅga*).

When the mind is sluggish, it is not the proper time for cultivating the following factors of enlightenment: tranquillity, concentration and equanimity, because a sluggish mind can hardly be aroused by them.

SN 45:53

When the mind is sluggish, it is the proper time for cultivating the following factors of enlightenment: investigation of reality, energy and rapture, because a sluggish mind can easily be aroused by them.

4. Contemplation of the spiritual journey

"I have to tread that path which the Buddhas, the Paccekabuddhas and the Great Disciples have gone; but by an indolent person that path cannot be trodden."

Vism IV.55

5. Contemplation of the Master's greatness

"Full application of energy was praised by my Master, and he is unsurpassed in his injunctions and a great help to us. He is honoured by practicing his Dhamma, not otherwise."

Ibid.

6. Contemplation on the greatness of the Heritage

"I have to take possession of the Great Heritage, called the Good Dhamma. But one who is indolent cannot take possession of it."

Ibid.

7. How to stimulate the mind

How does one stimulate the mind at a time when it needs stimulation? If due to slowness in the application of wisdom or due to non-attainment of the happiness of tranquillity, one's mind is dull, then one should rouse it through reflecting on the eight stirring objects. These eight are: birth, decay, disease and death; the suffering in the worlds of misery; the suffering of the past rooted in the round of existence; the suffering of the future rooted in the round of existence; the suffering of the present rooted in the search for food.

Vism IV.63

8. How to overcome sleepiness

Once the Exalted One spoke to the Venerable Mahā-Moggallāna thus: "Are you drowsy, Moggallāna? Are you drowsy, Moggallāna?"—"Yes, venerable sir."

(1) "Well then, Moggallāna, at whatever thought torpor has befallen you, to that thought you should not give attention, you should not dwell on it frequently. Then it is possible that, by so doing, torpor will disappear.

(2) "But if, by so doing, that torpor does not disappear, you should think and reflect within your mind about the Dhamma as you have heard and learned it, and you should mentally review it. Then it is possible that, by so doing, torpor will disappear.

(3) "But if, by so doing, that torpor does not disappear, you should learn by heart the Dhamma in its fullness, as you have heard and learned it. Then it is possible…

(4) "But if, by so doing, that torpor does not disappear, you should shake your ears, and rub your limbs with the palm of your hand. Then it is possible…

(5) "But if, by so doing, that torpor does not disappear, you should get up from your seat, and after washing your eyes with water, you should look around in all directions and look upwards to the stars in the sky. Then it is possible…

(6) "But if, by so doing, that torpor does not disappear, you should firmly establish the (inner) perception of light: as it is by day, so also by night; as it is by night, so also by day. Thus with a mind clear and

unobstructed, you should develop a consciousness which is full of brightness. Then it is possible…

(7) "But if, by so doing, that torpor does not disappear, you should, conscious of that which is before and behind, walk up and down, with your senses turned inwards, with your mind not going outwards. Then it is possible…

(8) "But if, by so doing, that torpor does not disappear, you may lie down on your right side, taking up the lion's posture, covering foot with foot—mindful, clearly conscious, keeping in mind the thought of rising. Having awakened again, you should quickly rise, thinking: 'I won't indulge in the enjoyment of lying down and reclining, in the enjoyment of sleep!'

"Thus, Moggallāna, you should train yourself!"

AN 7:58

9. The five threatening dangers

If, monks, a monk perceives these five threatening dangers, it is enough for him to live heedful, zealous, with a heart resolute to achieve the unachieved, to attain the unattained, to realize the unrealized. Which are these five dangers?

(1) Here, monks, a monk reflects thus: "I am now young, a youth, young in age, black-haired, in the prime of youth, in the first phase of life. But a time will come when this body will be in the grip of old age. But one who is overpowered by old age cannot easily contemplate on the Teachings of the Buddha; it is not easy for him to live in the wilderness or a forest or jungle, or in secluded dwellings. Before this undesirable condition,

so unpleasant and disagreeable, approaches me, prior to that, let me muster my energy for achieving the unachieved, for attaining the unattained, for realizing the unrealized, so that, in the possession of that state, I shall live happily even in old age."

(2) And further, monks, a monk reflects thus: "I am now free from sickness, free from disease, my digestive power functions smoothly, my constitution is not too cool and not too hot, it is balanced and fit for making effort. But a time will come when this body will be in the grip of sickness. And one who is sick cannot easily contemplate upon the Teachings of the Buddha; it is not easy for him, to live in the wilderness or a forest or jungle, or in secluded dwellings. Before this undesirable condition, so unpleasant and disagreeable, approaches me, prior to that, let me muster my energy for achieving the unachieved, for attaining the unattained, for realizing the unrealized, so that, in the possession of that state, I shall live happily even in sickness."

(3) And further, monks, a monk reflects thus: "Now there is an abundance of food, good harvests, easily obtainable is a meal of alms, it is easy to live on collected food and offerings. But a time will come when there will be a famine, a bad harvest, difficult to obtain will be a meal of alms, it will be difficult to live on collected food and offerings. And in a famine people migrate to places where food is ample, and there habitations will be thronged and crowded. But in habitations thronged and crowded one cannot easily contemplate upon the Teachings of the Buddha. Before this undesirable condition, so unpleasant and disagreeable,

approaches me, prior to that, let me muster my energy for achieving the unachieved, for attaining the unattained, for realizing the unrealized, so that, in the possession of that state, I shall live happily even in a famine."

(4) And further, monks, a monk reflects thus: "Now people live in concord and amity, in friendly fellowship as mingled milk and water and look at each other with friendly eyes. But there will come a time of danger, of unrest among the jungle tribes when the country people mount their carts and drive away and fear-stricken people move to a place of safety, and there habitations will be thronged and crowded. But in habitations thronged and crowded one cannot easily contemplate upon the Teachings of the Buddha. Before this undesirable condition, so unpleasant and disagreeable, approaches me, prior to that, let me muster my energy for achieving the unachieved, for attaining the unattained, for realizing the unrealized, so that, in the possession of that state, I shall live happily even in time of danger."

(5) And further, monks, a monk reflects thus: "Now the Congregation of Monks lives in concord and amity, without quarrel, lives happily under one teaching. But a time will come when there will be a split in the Congregation. And when the Congregation is split, one cannot easily contemplate upon the Teachings of the Buddha; it is not easy to live in the wilderness or a forest or jungle, or in secluded dwellings. Before this undesirable condition, so unpleasant and disagreeable, approaches me, prior to that, let me muster my energy

for achieving the unachieved, for attaining the unattained, for realizing the unrealized, so that, in the possession of that state, I shall live happily even when the Congregation is split."[3]

AN 5:78

These things, too, are helpful in conquering sloth and torpor:

1) Applied thought, of the factors of absorptions (*jhānaṅga*);
2) Energy, of the spiritual faculties (*indriya*);
3) Investigation of reality, energy and rapture, of the factors of enlightenment (*bojjhaṅga*).

When the mind is sluggish, it is not the proper time for cultivating the following factors of enlightenment: tranquillity, concentration and equanimity, because a sluggish mind can hardly be aroused by them.

When the mind is sluggish, it is the proper time for cultivating the following factors of enlightenment: investigation of reality, energy and rapture, because a sluggish mind can easily be aroused by them.

SN 46:53

---

3. This Discourse is one of the seven canonical texts recommended by the emperor Asoka in the Second Bhairat Rock Edict; "Reverend Sirs, these passages of the Law, to wit: ... 'Fears of what may happen (*anāgata-bhayāni*)..., spoken by the Venerable Buddha,—these, Reverend Sirs, I desire that many monks and nuns should frequently hear and meditate: and that likewise the laity, male and female, should do the same. (Vincent A. Smith, *Asoka*. 3rd ed., p. 54).

C. Simile

If there is a pot of water, covered with moss and water plants, then a man with a normal faculty of sight looking into it could not properly recognize and see the image of his own face. In the same way, when one's mind is possessed by sloth and torpor, overpowered by sloth and torpor, one cannot properly see the escape from sloth and torpor that have arisen; then one does not properly understand one's own welfare, nor that of another, nor that of both; and also texts memorized a long time ago do not come into one's mind, not to speak of those not memorized.

SN 46:55

Restlessness and Remorse

A. Nourishment of Restlessness and Remorse

There is unrest of mind; frequently giving unwise attention to it—that is the nourishment for the arising of restlessness and remorse that have not yet arisen, and for the increase and strengthening of restlessness and remorse that have already arisen.

SN 46:51

B. Denourishing of Restlessness and Remorse

There is quietude of mind; frequently giving wise attention to it—that is the denourishing of the arising of restlessness and remorse that have not yet arisen, and of the increase and strengthening of restlessness and remorse that have already arisen.

SN 46:51

Six things are conducive to the abandonment of restlessness and remorse:

1) Knowledge of the Buddhist scriptures (Doctrine and Discipline);
2) Asking questions about them;
3) Familiarity with the Vinaya (the Code of Monastic Discipline, and for lay followers, with the principles of moral conduct);
4) Association with those mature in age and experience, who possess dignity, restraint and calm;
5) Noble friendship;
6) Suitable conversation.

These things, too, are helpful in conquering restlessness and remorse:

1) Rapture, of the factors of absorption (*jhānaṅga*);
2) Concentration, of the spiritual faculties (*indriya*);
3) Tranquillity, concentration and equanimity, of the factors of enlightenment (*bojjhaṅga*).

When the mind is restless it is not the proper time for cultivating the following factors of enlightenment: investigation of the doctrine, energy and rapture, because an agitated mind can hardly be quietened by them.

When the mind is restless, it is the proper time for cultivating the following factors of enlightenment: tranquillity, concentration and equanimity, because an agitated mind can easily be quietened by them.

SN 46:53

C. Simile

If there is water in a pot, stirred by the wind, agitated, swaying and producing waves, a man with a normal faculty of sight could not properly recognize and see the image of his own face. In the same way, when one's mind is possessed by restlessness and remorse, overpowered by restlessness and remorse, one cannot properly see the escape from restlessness and remorse that have arisen; then one does not properly understand one's own welfare, nor that of another, nor that of both; and also texts memorized a long time ago do not come into one's mind, not to speak of those not memorized.

SN 46:55

Doubt

A. Nourishment of Doubt

There are things causing doubt; frequently giving unwise attention to them—that is the nourishment for the arising of doubt that has not yet arisen, and for the increase and strengthening of doubt that has already arisen.

SN 46:51

B. Denourishing of Doubt

There are things which are wholesome or unwholesome, blameless or blameworthy, noble or low, and (other) contrasts of dark and bright; frequently giving wise attention to them—that is the denourishing of the arising of doubt that has not yet arisen, and of the increase and strengthening of doubt that has already arisen.

Of the six things conducive to the abandonment of doubt, the first three and the last two are identical with those given for restlessness and remorse. The fourth is as follows:

1) Firm conviction concerning the Buddha, Dhamma and Sangha.
2) In addition, the following are helpful in conquering doubt:
3) Reflection, of the factors of absorption (*jhānaṅga*);
4) Wisdom, of the spiritual faculties (*indriya*);
5) Investigation of reality, of the factors of enlightenment (*bojjhaṅga*).

C. Simile

If there is a pot of water which is turbid, stirred up and muddy, and this pot is put into a dark place, then a man with a normal faculty of sight could not properly recognize and see the image of his own face. In the same way, when one's mind is possessed by doubt, overpowered by doubt, then one cannot properly see the escape from doubt which has arisen; then one does not properly understand one's own welfare, nor that of another, nor that of both; and also texts memorized a long time ago do not come into one's mind, not to speak of those not memorized.

SN 46:55

From the Sāmaññaphala Sutta

I. The Sutta (Dīgha Nikāya No. 2)

Being endowed with noble mindfulness and clear comprehension, and endowed with noble contentedness, the monk resorts to a lonely place: to a forest, the foot of a tree, a mountain, a cleft, a rock cave, a cemetery, a jungle, an open space, a heap of straw. After the meal, having returned from the alms-round, he sits down, crosslegged, keeping his body erect and his mindfulness alert. Having given up covetousness (= sensual desire) with regard to the world, he dwells with a heart free of covetousness, he cleanses his mind from covetousness. Having given up the blemish of ill-will, he dwells without ill-will; friendly and compassionate towards all living beings, he cleanses his mind from the blemish of ill-will. Having given up sloth and torpor, he dwells free from sloth and torpor, in the perception of light; mindful and clearly comprehending, he cleanses his mind from sloth and torpor. Having given up restlessness and remorse, he dwells without restlessness; his mind being calmed within, he cleanses it from restlessness and remorse. Having given up sceptical doubt, he dwells as one who has passed beyond doubt; being free from uncertainty about salutary things, he cleanses his mind from sceptical doubt.

Just as when a man taking a loan, engages in a trade, and his trade succeeds, he now not only disposes of his old debt but he has also, beyond that, a surplus for maintaining a wife. And at that he rejoices, is glad at heart…

Just as when a man is sick and in pain, suffering from a grave disease, his food does not agree with him, and he has no strength left in his body. But some time later he recovers from that sickness; he can again digest his food, and he regains his strength. And at that he rejoices, is glad at heart...

Just as when a man has been thrown into prison, but some time later he is released from prison; he is safe and without fears, and he did not suffer any loss of property. And at that he rejoices, is glad at heart...

Just as when a man is a slave, not independent, but dependent on others, unable to go where he likes, but some time later he is set free from slavery, is now independent, no longer dependent on others, a freeman who can go where he wants. And at that he rejoices, is glad at heart...

Just as when a man, rich and prosperous, travels through a wilderness where there is no food and much danger, but some time later he has crossed the desert, and gradually reaches safely the vicinity of a village, a place of safety, free from danger. And at that he rejoices, is glad at heart.

Similarly, so long as these five hindrances are not abandoned in him, a monk considers himself as indebted, as ailing, as imprisoned, as enslaved, as travelling in a wilderness.

But when these five hindrances are abandoned, he considers himself as free from debt, rid of illness, emancipated from the prison's bondage, as a free man, and as one arrived at a place of safety.

And when he sees himself free of these five hindrances, joy arises; in him who is joyful, rapture arises; in him whose mind is enraptured, the body is stilled; the body being stilled, he feels happiness; and a happy mind finds concentration.

Then detached from sensual desires, detached from unwholesome states, he enters into and dwells in the first absorption which is accompanied by applied thought and reflection, born of detachment, and filled with joy and rapture. He enters into and dwells in the second… third… fourth absorption.

II. The Commentary

A. The Similes for the Hindrances

The text of the discourse says: "Similarly, so long as these five hindrances are not abandoned in him, a monk considers himself as indebted, as ailing, as imprisoned, as enslaved, as travelling in a wilderness."

Hereby the Blessed One shows the unabandoned hindrance of sensual desire as similar to being in debt; and the other hindrances as similar to being ill, and so on. These similes should be understood as follows:

1. Sensual Desire

There is a man who has incurred a debt but has become ruined. Now, if his creditors, when telling him to pay back the debt, speak roughly to him or harass and beat him, he is unable to retaliate but has to bear it all. It is his debt that causes this forbearance.

In the same way, if a man is filled with sensual desire for a certain person, he will, full of craving for that object of his desire, be attached to it. Even if spoken to roughly by that person, or harassed or beaten, he will bear it all. It is his sensual desire that causes this forbearance. In that way, sensual desire is like being in debt.

2. Ill-Will

If a man suffers from a bilious disease, and receives even honey and sugar, he will not enjoy its flavour, owing to his bile sickness; he will just vomit it, complaining, "It is bitter, bitter!"

In the same way, if one of angry temperament is admonished even slightly by his teacher or preceptor who wishes his best, he does not accept their advice. Saying "You harass me too much!" he will leave the Order, or go away and roam about. Just as the bilious person does not enjoy the flavour of honey and sugar, so one who has the disease of anger will not enjoy the taste of the Buddha's Dispensation consisting in the happiness of the meditative absorptions, etc. In that way, ill-will resembles illness.

3. Sloth and Torpor

A person has been kept in jail during a festival day, and so could see neither the beginning nor the middle nor the end of the festivities. If he is released on the following day, and hears people saying: "Oh, how delightful was yesterday's festival! Oh, those dances and songs!" he will not give any reply. And why not? Because he did not enjoy the festival himself.

Similarly, even if a very eloquent sermon on the Dhamma is going on, a monk overcome by sloth and torpor will not know the beginning, middle or end. If after the sermon, he hears it praised: "How pleasant was it to listen to the Dhamma! How interesting was the topic and how good the similes!" he will not be able to say a word. And why not? Because, owing to his sloth and torpor, he did not enjoy the sermon. In that way, sloth and torpor are comparable to imprisonment.

4. Restlessness and Remorse

A slave who wants to enjoy himself at a festival is told by his master: "Go quickly to such and such a place! There is urgent work to do. If you don't go, I shall have your hands and feet cut off, or your ears and nose!" Hearing that, the slave will quickly go as ordered, and will not be able to enjoy any part of the festival. This is because of his dependence on others.

Similarly it is with a monk not well versed in the Vinaya (the Disciplinary Code), who has gone to the forest for the sake of solitude. If in any matter, down to the question of permissible meat (Sub-Cy: e.g., pork) he gets the idea that it was not permissible (taking it for bear's flesh), he has to interrupt his solitude and, to purify his conduct, has to go to one skilled in the Vinaya. Thus he will not be able to enjoy the happiness of solitude because of his being overcome by restlessness and remorse. In that way, restlessness and remorse are like slavery.

5. Sceptical Doubt

A man travelling through a desert, aware that travellers may be plundered or killed by robbers, will, at the mere sound of a twig or a bird, become anxious and fearful, thinking: "The robbers have come!" He will go a few steps, and then out of fear, he will stop, and continue in such a manner all the way; or he may even turn back. Stopping more frequently than walking, only with toil and difficulty will he reach a place of safety, or he may not even reach it.

It is similar with one in whom doubt has arisen in regard to one of the eight objects of doubt.[4] Doubting whether the Master is an Enlightened One or not, he cannot accept it in confidence, as a matter of trust. Unable to do so, he does not attain to the paths and fruits of sanctity. Thus, as the traveller in the desert is uncertain whether robbers are there or not, he produces in his mind, again and again, a state of wavering and vacillation, a lack of decision, a state of anxiety; and thus he creates in himself an obstacle for reaching the safe ground of sanctity (*ariya-bhūmi*). In that way, sceptical doubt is like travelling in a desert.

B. The Abandonment of the Hindrances

The text of the Discourse says:

"But when these five hindrances are abandoned, the monk considers himself as free from debt, rid of illness, emancipated from the prison's bondage, as a free man, and as one arrived at a place of safety."

1. The Abandonment of Sensual Desire

A man, having taken a loan, uses it for his business and comes to prosperity. He thinks: "This debt is a cause of vexation." He returns the loan together with the interest, and has the promissory note torn up. After that he neither sends a messenger nor a letter to his creditors; and even if he meets them it depends on

4. They are, according to the Vibhaṅga: doubt in regard to the Buddha, the Dhamma, the Sangha, the (threefold) training, the past, the future, both past and future, and the conditionality of phenomena dependently arisen.

his wish whether he will get up from his seat to greet them, or not. And why? He is no longer in debt to them or dependent of them.

Similarly, a monk thinks: "Sensual desire is a cause of obstruction." He then cultivates the six things leading to its abandonment, and removes the hindrance of sensual desire. Just as one who has freed himself of debt no longer feels fear or anxiety when meeting his former creditors, so one who has given up sensual desire is no longer attached and bound to the object of his desire; even if he sees divine forms, passions will not assail him.

Therefore the Blessed One compared the abandonment of sensual desire to freedom from debt.

2. *The Abandonment of Ill-Will*

Just as a person suffering from a bilious disease, having been cured by taking medicine, will regain his taste for honey and sugar, similarly a monk, thinking, "This ill-will causes much harm," develops the six things leading to its abandonment and removes the hindrance of ill-will. Just as the cured patient partaking of honey and sugar appreciates the taste, so also this monk receives with reverence the rules of training, and observes them with appreciation (of their value). Therefore the Blessed One compared the abandonment of ill-will to the recovery of health.

3. *The Abandonment of Sloth and Torpor*

There is a person that once had been in jail on a festival day. But when freed and celebrating the festival on a later occasion, he will think: "Formerly, through the fault of my heedlessness, I was in prison on that day and could not enjoy this festival. Now I shall be heedful." And he remains heedful of his conduct so that nothing detrimental finds entry into his mind. Having enjoyed the festival, he exclaims: "Oh, what a beautiful festival it was!"

Similarly a monk, perceiving that sloth and torpor do great harm, develops the six things opposed to them, and so removes the hindrance of sloth and torpor. Just as the man freed from prison enjoys the whole length of the festival, even for seven days, so this monk who has given up sloth and torpor is capable of enjoying the beginning, the middle and the consummation of the Festival of the Dhamma (*dhamma-nakkhatta*), and finally attains to Arahatship together with the fourfold discriminating knowledge (*paṭisambhidā*)

Therefore the Blessed One spoke of the abandonment of sloth and torpor as being comparable to release from imprisonment.

4. The Abandonment of Restlessness and Remorse

There is a slave who, with the help of a friend, pays money to his master, becomes a free man, and is henceforth able to do what he likes. Similarly a monk, perceiving the great obstruction caused by restlessness and remorse, cultivates the six things opposed to them, and thus gives up restlessness and remorse. And having given them up, he is like a truly free man, able to do as he wishes. Just as no one can forcibly stop a free man from doing what he likes, so can restlessness and remorse no longer stop that monk from walking the happy path of renunciation (*sukha-nekkhamma-paṭipadā*).

Therefore the Blessed One declared the abandonment of restlessness and remorse as being similar to winning freedom from slavery.

5. The Abandonment of Sceptical Doubt

There is a strong man who, with his luggage in hand and well armed, travels through a wilderness in company. If robbers see him even from afar, they will take flight. Crossing safely the wilderness and reaching a place of safety, he will rejoice in his safe arrival. Similarly a monk, seeing that sceptical doubt is a cause of great harm, cultivates the six things that are its antidote, and gives up doubt. Just as that strong man, armed and in company, taking as little account of the robbers as of the grass on the ground, will safely come out of the wilderness to a safe place; similarly a monk, having crossed the wilderness of evil conduct, will finally reach the state of highest security, the deathless realm of Nibbāna. Therefore the Blessed One compared the abandonment of sceptical doubt to reaching a place of safety.

THE BUDDHIST PUBLICATION SOCIETY

The BPS is an approved charity dedicated to making known the Teaching of the Buddha, which has a vital message for all people.

Founded in 1958, the BPS has published a wide variety of books and booklets covering a great range of topics. Its publications include accurate annotated translations of the Buddha's discourses, standard reference works, as well as original contemporary expositions of Buddhist thought and practice. These works present Buddhism as it truly is—a dynamic force which has influenced receptive minds for the past 2500 years and is still as relevant today as it was when it first arose.

For more information about the BPS and our publications, please visit our website, or write an e-mail, or a letter to the:

Administrative Secretary
Buddhist Publication Society
P.O. Box 61
54 Sangharaja Mawatha
Kandy • Sri Lanka
E-mail: bps@bps.lk
web site: http://www.bps.lk
Tel: 0094 81 223 7283 • Fax: 0094 81 222 3679